[EMINENT DOMAIN]

[EMINENT DOMAIN]

Justin Petropoulos

MARSH HAWK PRESS

East Rockaway, New York • 2011

11 12 13 14 15   7 6 5 4 3 2 1   First Edition

Marsh Hawk Press books are published by Poetry Mailing List, Inc.,
a not-for-profit corporation under section 501 (c) 3
United States Internal Revenue Code.

Cover and interior art by Manny Prieres from "Falling Series."
Cover and interior design by Claudia Carlson.
Author photograph by Beril Gulcan.
The text and display are set in Bembo and Bembo Book.

Library of Congress Cataloging-in-Publication Data

Petropoulos, Justin.
Eminent domain / Justin Petropoulos. -- 1st ed.
     p. cm.
ISBN-13: 978-0-9841177-9-6 (<pbk>)
ISBN-10: 0-9841177-9-2 (<pbk>)
I. Title.
PS3616.E8676E45 2011
811'.6--dc22
                                    2010046791

Marsh Hawk Press
P.O. Box 206, East Rockaway, N.Y. 11518-0206
www.marshhawkpress.org

Acknowledgements

The author gratefully acknowledges the editors of the following publications, in which some of the poems herein first appeared, sometimes in slightly different form: *A cappella Zoo, American Letters & Commentary, Anemone Sidecar, Borderlands: Texas Poetry Review, Columbia Poetry Review, Crab Creek Review, Gulf Coast, Mandorla, MiPOesias, Portland Review and Suss: Another Literary Journal.*

Thanks to Sandy McIntosh, Thomas Fink, Claudia Carlson and everyone at Marsh Hawk Press for all their hard work and careful stewardship of this collection. Thank you Anne Waldman for this tremendous honor.

These poems where informed and shaped by the insight and generosity of Ellen Wehle, Campbell McGrath, Catherine Bowman, David Wojahn, Kevin Young, Manuel Luis Martinez, Jon Bowman, Vivek Borey, Susan Briante, Yago Cura, Julia Gordon, J. David Gonzalez, N.S. Koenings, Heather Madden, Dan Manchester, Kevin Marzahl, Loyal Miles, Sara Jane Stoner, David Ramm, Julie Story and Anthony Tognazzini. Thank you all so much for your guidance and support for these poems and me.

Special thanks to Simeon Berry and Paul Martinez Pompa, this collection belongs to you—every word.

para meus pais com todo o meu amor

Contents

EMINENT DOMAIN

1. COINCIDENCE OF WANTS

1.01

It must be said from the outset that economies of affection have nothing to do with fondness, per se. Rather, they connote. Some of us wave to the soldiers. A contract housing a colony, a storefront of sweet things. Whether it was guava seeds or a transfiguration is unclear. Mattock, precordium, a colander of condensed milk. The impatience of Super-NOW accounts. Anything you can say savored for itself, alone. But the collector node reflects the amount of evidence collected in support of belief (disbelief) in a given relation.

I only remember the prayer for snakes. If you say the words through your nose the snakes disappear, lassoed off by the wind. Already a microphone crosses the threshold of lips, echoes — those debts — slipped interior. The way his hair always smacked wisteria or the treasury buys spools of copper for subsidiary currency from a foreign multinational. Each coil fed through a blanketing press. Punching out zygotes. Surrounded by callused tissue, not only memories, but the distances in their refrain.

At this *here* rate, always running toward a starting gun. Fire recoils along morning's cables. Smoke lilts from the bus as its doors fold open. Coughed up passengers — most of us work here — passing along the conveyer to the furnace. But even saints are depicted with their hands turned toward themselves. Armed with compasses, circling so to speak. You know, I never go out in the rain anymore. There's a honey locust outside, wilted to the thorns. That's why the prayers are secret.

1.02

The doors are ajar with a sudden awareness: we can be easily moved. Small parking lot, that particular slouching. Seeds swallowed shameless, away. These are the excuses. Talk to me.

But our current vogue for *non* continues; a disembodied whistling almost in every town. Larger particles (10 micrometers roughly) dashed against cotton. The vulgar phosphorus agitated by the attrition of a glowworm rushing from a glass, that currents against your finger.

I remember you, remember you saying, "let's begin lesson one." All you knew of dreaming. Newts darting, newts at rest.

1.03

You're at the door yoked to something dead. Its hooves as you breathe like typewriters. Eventually we are no closer to the weather. Only four when the gasoline leaked in. Humidity buckled the duct-taped windows, a fussed, fast mooring. Our small breaths as quantities of wool denoted here by (x) decreasing in each sweater (y) at a rate inversely proportional to the skin.

Designed as a companion product decreasing acoustic transmissions, the border zone locked with protesters. Static eyed station after station. Skeletal buildings teeter. They flipped a car. It's on fire now. And who do you suppose is going to pay for all this? Agglomeration of foreign direct investment usually makes the roof heavier. Promise me something, if only to promise me something—described from its girders and when.

1.04

To keep warm you made spectacle of an orange. Having been recognized, kaolin erodes. As to the feeling of having on the one hand. Clinging disparately to our limits. We burned cornhusks in the stove, curled ourselves around the smoke. So to speak. An elaborate series of pulleys speeds the pocked, hemorrhagic bucket up. Confetti arcs from a thresher. Our lungs dissolve it in mucus and sweep it away. Into the sun each morning someone is found. Missing, not wholly themselves. Knife, rind, a galaxy held together by a thumb, a price index. We rely on tradition, on passing by the sides of bodies. Two little thermometers suspended so as not to touch.

1.05

Sky pinned open in a wax tray. Abdominal diagram.
Reconfiguration of a dandelion. Any vertigo blown through.
Milk production, notwithstanding the toll, will lose what
existed, the act of *going by,* itself.

The expense of transporting one part of the city to another will
increase. All these heavy goods proportioned to the tonnage
of light. The production of windows, the speediest most
effectual remedy for coughs, will slow. Even the cough will
assemble slower. The throat for all such goods, consequently,
will narrow.

Any taxonomy advanced by a carrier is thus inflationary.
Shelled. Her feet signify and seed an economy blown across
a border, barbed, definitive. Say it please, like a kidney boxed
in dry ice.

1.06

Iguanas pendant, tails clasped from branches. Stomachs flushed, pooled beneath their bodies, mouths rigor-locked, exclaiming. Commercial traffic secretes translations of an organ grinder's arm as it breathes its crank. Lesions at this stage have a split pea's proportions in the lungs. The halls molt. This desire extends, arresting the terms of our contract. Each clause is factorial, hatched in a bread bag factory, and circuits the cracks in our shells. Currency organized by lucid bodies. Among the newly born, glancing together in the center of a room, insulation retires to a fine power, is swept. Vacancy exceeds itself. A man dancing or a chair.

2. EMINENT DOMAIN

2.01

The quick of a train, cut to the quick. Locomotion unpacked into points on a map. We sleep, a trampled chain of paper dolls, nested in each other's hair. An apple, chewed past the seeds, wobbles away from its mark, from where they dragged him away. Like the others. Blankets buckled like molted skins.

"Just as you arrive there, you ask for the house of Mr. Y," my mother told me before leaving. "They will show you the way." But what is topography, if not a dream of palming mountains?

When Mr. Y saw me, he told me that he was convinced that I had died. "Because I heard that you vanished, that prescriptions resolved your lungs." The inference, that stumbling leads to falling can felicitously be transferred to the abstract domain of economic policy. "These scars," that man did oft remark, "are but tokens."

With the advent of paper currency, trouser pockets grew smaller, hands fell quickly from fashion. Now archaic, the quick, quickens. Chemicals, similar to tactile apprehension, deposit in the same tissues as calcium. He calculated strontium-90's rate of turnover within the body, pointed me to the house of Mr. X. "He will recognize you before too long."

I walk passed a chorus of crickets chirping at Polaris. Through a flimsy curtain, I see Mr. X hunkered over someone, a woman, almost completely out of frame. He whispers to her. People say she was different after that. Possessed by the sadness with a beak. But I'm still not sure that he spoke, that I heard anything except his breathing and the rasp of someone's joints behind me.

2.02

When you dress, it is not immaterial. The order you perform. The operations. When in dressing you start with the shirt and end with the coat, then in undressing you observe. First, take off the coat and the shirt comes last.

We are now enmeshed in complex questions of timing. A school district with a single salary schedule faces a perfectly elastic supply curve for physics teachers. A mapping (s) of space associates with every space point (p) a point (~p) as its image. A special such mapping is the identity (i) carrying every point (p) into itself.

The pictures recoil from the plaster, afraid to wake, they just give in, whimper against the floor. In theory, the flash could blind us. A man squawks heel to toe, in place, as if he feels gravitation's syllables in cuts of sugarcane girdled in chicken wire. Its possible. If we're guilty, who cares? They got rid of us. Couldn't fit us into their categories. What kind of refugee escapes in a car and thus collapses in an orgy of inconvertible note issues?

During the subsequent devaluation, you told me the bowler was derived from a medieval helmet emblazoned with an elephant draped in lilies. "They protect the psychology," you said, "from the burdensome draft, deflecting the occasional blow." Crows corkscrew from the treetops, brawl for their limbs. The air is full of limestone and sparks that flint from a dragging muffler. So you see, I don't need wallpaper to make me sad. You arrive first as sound, body being too much for you to bare.

2.03

Tethered to a counterwork of *here/say*, we fold ourselves inside, lick this jaundiced postage, commute ourselves. We drudge through the oleanders, reflective objects in an otherwise chalk, closer than we appear, only typeset farther apart.

They have stopped bussing the tables, stopped sweeping. Bodies under the proverbial. Lint pressed, this disupholstery of somewhere, of dried apricots, rationed by weight. So invested, we never occurred to each other. But what can we give a child of empire? Something discursive, that won't leave them. Prosthetics in the land of dreams.

At this *here* rate there will be no bruise. Ocher watermark sutured instead to a galvanized pipe. Phantom syntax, still tangled, caresses morning's flimsy coat. Bodies long gone in the sleeves. Like a whisper. We wash each other's hands.

[digression on the corn trade]

When the corn flops, he zips it open and says *corn*, affixing
its exchange rate to the dollar in the pocket of a pair of pants
walking legless through a constantly compounding sentence,
whose demands fuel inflation, whose meaning expands with
just enough velocity to keep from re-collapsing. The upsetting
machine rolls a familiar umbilical edge.

Drain cover screws, plaqued mint. He routes his nose in a
bouquet of gasoline soaked rags. Handfuls, in the dark. It's only
dangerous if he trains on a flint. He wanders off. Sometimes to
the boiler room to make a wish: blotting paper soaked across
pilots. A whisper or a building unlights the fog. Prostrate,
static, a bundled fragment pressuring its surround.

2.04

When the question of abductions is put to them, they say
cardamom, ground thumb. Ellipses followed by galoshes with
no referent. Umbrellas grommet the street. Issued against
the tumbling ash. Rumors, of children gone missing in the
cedars, returned with their eyes thatched, of someone garroted.
Reporters arrive, receding. Sunlight swabs the mattress where
its springs have withdrawn to accommodate that sleeping part
of you shaped like a lima bean.

In the border zone, a healthy pair of corneas is worth more
than half a year's wages. You are nothing if not plain spoken.
Shimmering, stained, 80 people dead or dying, traced back
to a singular point of departure, only greyer. At the cellular
level, our bodies interpret, interrupt an oleander's supple
circumferences, however poisonous. Screen doors, torn from
their frames used as stretchers in each night's procession.

2.05

In a shop window, a tailor hems a mannequin's fennel suit. Takes in the trousers. He is bent, cursing his ankles, by a dim light, which pleats slowly the alley where a woman catches rain. She drifts slightly, eyes closed. Swabbed from a wound. Clouds toweled over an arm of dogwoods. Plotted in that tractrix of branches, cardinals coo. The existing government barricades itself in the capital building. Sandbag by sandbag city compels ocean. Sand is now the currency of choice for domestic investiture. Sometime later, the tailor, mid-seam, is spirited away. Through a gauntlet of checkpoints, night stutters its blue sentence in the side view mirror. The horizon line disfigured, confessing.

[digression on the corn trade]

A peanut vendor sleeps beneath our uncanny resemblances, chews the brim of an old hat made of cellophane, near the gates. A refugee camp should be setup on sloped terrain that provides natural drainage.

Someone will discover her there, as if she were a theory or its half versed deck of flashcards. This is an economy of light weapons—you know: it remembers nothing about its course. Some sell part of their rations for rice, at the expense of caloric intake. Scurvy is a constant. Strangers pass a blush grown through quietly. Mission bells with grass. Spongiform, the refinery bloats. Phyllode or nematode, as with us a chance cleaving.

"If you build your boat from this, it will float," she promised them, with a blowzy stonefly and fire-eater's tremble, extending them a weight of seed in her palm. In exchange, they offered odes to point/non-point source pollution, runoff: bits of hair and salt, manure, slurry of paper dolls flushed from the mine. "It's not a question of food, he said. "If we had the chance, we would walk even tonight."

As the corn grows a girl scrapes jacks by twos followed by pink impacts. Bread bags caucus. We collect the copper jackets now, lozenges nested in the mud-throats of loons. Melt them down. Beyond the fence a scorched earth policy town sutured by a lattice of clotheslines.

3. NIGHT OF FAILED AUTOPSIES

3.01

Fennel pretends at being a scarf, its bottle stung with dust and further. Drain the excess into or assign to a subsidiary. We stand aside as he pries the maw free and wraps it in a piece of blue cotton he never tears from his shirt. You found him particular, slouching under a dogwood.

Night of failed autopsies in a small parking lot she runs her fingers through. Trout and slate, soaked into their clothes. That disquiet, for a long time. There has been erosion between nation-states and convenience-oriented packaging, mutual cannibalization. Stopped by the patrols, coupons avalanche from her pockets, each a memorial, perforated.

Steel guitar issues from a tumbledown phonograph. You pressed the stamp to your tongue, face down, tracing it to his weakest rib. But who keeps receipts anymore? Let's say this man from a certain longitude abducts children from the periphery. Supposing the horizontal.

Parallax of the news cycle is twelve seconds. The children's families have already had their days in court—a wet cleaning. Like clockwork, she walloped a mop with each new sun in sour abatement of the buckwheat groat, growing denser by degrees, not to a point, but a bending. We mark time: every train station ago. Our bodies parsed down to the fingernails. The glue is almost sweet.

3.02

We shared a certain ire, capillarity in our digits. Her finger was too thick for the maze, however. Even angled, it obscures. With her fingernail, she machetes backward through the maze, outward from the center toward the edge, crumbs those pages into fists, a magnifying glass.

She remembers, as a child, counting pebbles into a conch by the shore. Knuckle by knuckle. Everything is reversible in this narrow sense of holding. Thus space (economy) at any time is a special aspect (purely substitutional) perhaps aiming to recover the moon. She rubs it with a little oil or white of an egg to fill the scratches. Hedgerows at dusk make off with her silhouette, a second skin secreted from without her self invisibly. Cicadas all summer like silence.

3.03

So close to the fire. We could taste the jasmine. Palm oil faces of people once. Those posters of the missing or dead haunt the streets no matter how hard we sweep. Reams of them overexposed. They clutched at her arms from signposts.

Outside the camp, fresh tar wrinkles behind convoys of copper trucks. They sound as if towed by geese. She remembers her first miracle: window after window after the voices under all that glass. Stories coffin those bodies. Disappeared. We pry each bent nail from their roving.

Near money seeds the sale of simple, negentropic valences. Their pursuit, silently, from the bulldozer's exhaustoria. Pearls. The tide purls. We are remainders, disaggregate, encoded bone. Our narrative tires. Despite this contrary bed, linens imply a body abandoned. Cinderblocks. Teeth half pulled.

3.04

A martial-style curfew whispers across the city. Street lights strobe through a stand of dogwoods, barely in bloom. The ambulance service ceases. They listen intently to the rumors. Relax; remember to breathe. Mopping up operations are underway. The price of corn has achieved record-breaking proportions. Your troubles disperse like soapsuds, grenades splintering windows. But if you act calm, you will be calm. A suitcase decorates your hand; cigarette casts your orange face off into orbit. You keep no memories of him—he is weightless—only dragonflies, hundreds, stitching their wings inside that case where you always go to hide.

3.05

We set fires. Water them. Hide from flies in the smoke. Carbon burned from bodies will be used in the next great paving. A girl draws sewers into the strects with chalk, whispers directions between the grates. Each sentence: song and needle and the vinyl spinning. Water mains with glamorous rifling. A parting shot echoes, syntactic, at each intersection.

Absorbing strontium-90, (the lack of what has gone by) plants ramble beneath their potting (sidewalks) contaminated with this way not that. After crossing the river, traces of the journey are eaten by dairy cows. What remains is the lender of last resort, a bridge and the hope that these apparitions won't forfeit your weight.

4. Homing Instincts

4.01

I watched a man reverse-engineer a light bulb once. Right in front of me! But all its characters had out-turned feet, were confused by buttons of varying luminosities. These embryos were put through an edge-rolling operation in the upsetting machine. This process gives them the familiar umbilical edge. It also makes it easier to automatically feed them. I guess there are properties and then there are properties. I love to watch the neighbors' fences burn. The umbilical edge hardens during the upsetting process, thereby preventing the soft cranium from squirting between the collar during stamping. Bacteria, however, are fooled easily from their homing instincts and so, as a precaution, I put a bucket of water on the table for us, to dampen our frequency, to quench our thirst along the way.

4.02

You have been following crickets around with a special napkin for opening doors. Regressive taxes on profits are applied where applicable. Furniture careens in empty houses. Supposing the horizontal. Not to a point, but a bending mop (rather than a broom) in sour abatement of our debris. You will have spent the night in a field setting a camera flash off in your eyes.

Patrols like puffers, a scaled inflation, to narrow the consequence of busses. He carries his money rolled in his throat. His shirt collar starched secret. The sun hangs its however, a laundry of reds, above a pack of strays which scratch through barrels bloated with buckwheat groat.

But in my memory, you are always in soft focus, sand in your hair, talking about ghosts, the blue and white trucks that came for your sister in the night. You clear the autumn drains with a ladle. Fluorescent dye maps your sentence through karst towers and my hair is not long enough to be rescued.

4.03

Hauling up anchor, a ship, even in drifting, remains huge. The vertical is saddened by the horizontal's constant expectation of footsteps. Nearing the bathtub, she drives nails into the exposed fiberglass. Garbage cans twist and carry on, hitched to the bumper of a bus, which coordinates past her huckleberry yard. Amen.

It's summer. Leaves eaten to lace, which is all the rage with the theater set, those monologues with hands, dreaming. Alas there is nothing. A stranger's stories sustain us. We are caterpillars, all. At least that's what I've been told. In the mean time, I've got a basement. It floods.

4.04

This morning people have been uncovering manholes, breathing that air. A woman with swollen fingers of un-shucked corn in a thin wire basket walks as if under water. Yes, the two men were dressed in civilian clothes, but that doesn't mean they're not military. I tried to visit you at home but lost my rule for governing intersections. After that, I began to receive threats. There is a picture going around of a cloned sheep titled: Undesirables.

They wanted to question someone. Came for me in the morning with an empty birdcage. Made me knock on your door, as if seeing me, neighbor, you'd open-up, offer us tea. Feet shuffle, cars pop like bubbles — prudishly deionized. I knock three more times. The hallway chipped clean to the fiberglass like an ulcer.

When we returned they wore their military clothes. Waves in the distance curling to shore like a beaver's claws around a tree limb where termites work the wood hollow enough for the wind to whistle through. It was night. I called out your name. As the light breached the door they told me to go home. And I tried. Chalk settled in my fingertips, but nothing out there would float. Tomorrow it will be my turn: someone at the door begging a cup of tea or salt. Close your eyes and I'll let you in.

5. PASSIVE VOICE

5.01

It seems we will starve, first the moths then me. I can see the chapel dusty through the glass: thin blue doors, gargoyle eating its own wing. But our window is a fixative, six cents worth, and for me it dries always the same.

The man who rings the bell refuses to shake hands with a stranger, trailing herself with salt. He works his shadow into something guilty like a comet. "Tell me a story with smoke in its eyes," he says. "Tell me moths quiet the walls." She forgives him. She knows he conspires rarely with people, having lived too long haunted by the memory of a millipede dragging its back legs across a scarf.

5.02

In the evening, you compared people who would not dream of making noise. Their faces encaustic, shot hollow, waltzing. You must believe we are too. Turn by turn there is nothing. Trailing ourselves with salt, too old for our mouths, etc: committed to that proposition.

But can there be retching with no body to contract certain protocols (re-suspensions) that suggest a standardized completely decorative aspect of time? You are propelled through the spire crossing by what was spun behind. A martial-style curfew oxidizes. "Breath isn't invisible," you say. "It's scaffolding."

I found pictures of the wasp's nest you unbuckled from the window. Within the architecture of nation-state, borders (loading systems) respond to each payload separately, establish makeshift housing. Growth of algae, decay of algae, your breath blouses, falls away.

5.03

The tanks roll. Heavy tread culls, learning the ground like muscles forgetting. Three men read aloud from a smoke damaged carpet. She is above him, a crane, whichever kind, costuming his wound with gauze. The roof of her home peeled. They rifled her closets, monitored calls, interrogated her friends. She watched, metonymized, a waltz seared in her springs, measuring the time between seeing a raindrop and its collision. Above the city, a city disappears and the wind asks after the rest. Strangers pass a blush, grown through with grass and quiet. Mission bells. A second autumn of shirts buttoned in the branches. Shivers waiting for bodies.

5.04

The sun sets in the spine. She turns the page and misspells his eyes, scours her inseam with orange peels in the dark, but she doesn't recognize his fingers. He steams from her, basically, like thymine. A second skin secreted from without herself.

Invisibly the statement follows by induction. When considering that there exists an ordering such that the variable (n) denotes the dimension of the corresponding complex space. Let's take for example the word inter( )ment.

A room balloons. Beyond its sills, border patrols convey our isosceles comings and goings toward a perfectly elastic supply curve for labor under the guise of a national agricultural initiative. The other day I watched a woman work soil from stone and even my cough assembled slower. Our relief tendered from a single glacier. All this rain transgressing, called back into being and being lost.

They give us everything here. I would be eating crow if I complained. They are kind, feed us. But I spend hours arranging peppercorns: stick figures in the throws of a waltz, a pair of spectacles. I had my own orchard. I miss it. Here we are just pacing. We chew cured beef, dried apricots, sleep a bit, and talk. We are talking so much.

5.05

Praying into your shirt's starched collar, a letter crumbed from your hands and I know now that busses are made from what the sparrows left behind. The sun hangs its laundry, a however of reds, in soft focus, across a transparency of snow.

Carnations are pinned to a class of boys sentenced to die, each flower, sewing for water in their jackets. The desired target gap value may be achieved by diversifying among individuals (securities) of different but offsetting durations. A shot is fired from the left barrel of a double barrel shot gun, the object hit by that shot. Both are called left. A sparrow-bill maker splinters nails from an iron rod. Liters of sparks faucet from her window.

I cough in the morning, cough morning completely. You know, that light sharpened through the tip of an icicle, fence line steeped into lake. Sometimes in the deceptions: water, throat, memory, there is a song, yellow-pale wearing against the granite where we crave the salt of gulls. Where we evacuate by degrees.

Today I heard a man say that history would judge him, as if history were not like winter. Sink framed with tea bags, some dry, others like snow. Perfect.

5.06

Tired by now, feet anchoring along, by the presence of a now, by so much walking on this loose earth. We follow a passage like an eel. The number of people living in a camp depends on the crisis. Sometimes the blast bears skin no register. Nevertheless organs: pressed, white butterflies.

Streetlights strobe, fractured by still trees — is still an equation whose efficacies disclose as functions of political power. In this case, aid agencies look to improve the camp or the population should be moved elsewhere. Bicycles keel and he begins. To unknot the moon. Small. Lanterns tucked in the branches.

The vertical prays on the horizontal's constant expectation of footsteps. Their embargoed tendons pulverized in a thermos. Packed with dry ice. An old man buries a wreath of gladiolas. His hand, aware of us, waves handsome. Tailpipe, teakettle, breadth, hands that are, sometimes, the sincerest freight. Someone breaks toward the alley. To buy time. Evening trains debate their tracks. The monetary system corrects its borders.

Light blisters from these point objects. Recognizes like alcohol. In this specific, statistical sense, they are a kind of clock: timing coils, tool bitten, as if dimensionality (an efficient workforce) exists in fractions, in the successive ticks of our particulars.

5.07

Now here is this mob. Strangers, you know. There is a difference in appearance, in the way we walk. A peculiar speechlessness in the face of the national and international organizations, whose object of care and control we are. She walks as someone who is about to fall over. One would say she is extremely tired. When he walks, the street is his. You'd say he's walking on eggs, afraid to crash.

Not that long ago they killed a decent boy nearby. No wonder everyone is against them. Curses them in the factory. Our accounts are disqualified almost a priori. The government set up a proper camp for them. I told my wife, soon they'll be eating better than us.

Prosthetic languages. To lay claim to. Production of authoritative narratives about migrant populations is, no matter how difficult to swallow, a growth industry. Suspicious about everything, he is like someone who doesn't feel like living anymore. They rebelled you know. We said. We told you. Let the barbarians in and this is what you get for thanks.

He will be looking 100 meters ahead of us — look there — someone who is afraid that maybe he will be caught. Imagine, meat every day, in these hard times.

5.08

Face down in the snow, a man says, "This is the smell of the sky." He is a medium, a coordinate. Snow melts into the crows of his eyes, giving over the water already always implied. "I have these amethysts," I say, opening my hand, "flossed from dentures lost at sea by shouting sailors."

Our talk leads to speculation: soybeans all lit up with frost, hunters quack from an unknowable distance, a woman packs her car with snow, but nothing else will come to shore, for certain, except more shore.

"I miss all of my ducks," I say. "Their isosceles comings and goings." As I touch his arm thin under all that fabric his body turns away from the clock, which fringes the city. "The edge," he says, "is the center of something else and I am running away from there."

He stuffs my hand in his pocket; a pigeon, also stuffed, wrestles my fingers. "This is not a duck," I say. "I'll give you five dollars, though, for the bones." Looking into my hand, he asks for an amethyst, the coldest one, with his shoulders. Ice flows shrinking from a glacier — please.

6. THE CITY BEAUTIFUL

6.01

When we say move over — protuberant hacking spooled
tight with suppressant syrups — do we always mean on a tin
spoon for the cameras? Balloons evaporate into the crowd.
Bench moored, slanted to a spruce. Both of us burned. Quite.
Cumulous. Blue baby splashed with rose water. Downed ash
in the doctor's lungs. His foot an alloy of copper dust and boot
leather. Ulcerous. Herons paper and unpaper wings.

Too often we reason in dichotomies, strapped at the waist to
an iron kettle set on coals. Mosquitoes like high voltage power
lines siren in the mangroves. Fishermen marionette from the
water. Their joints infectious with pause. We steam orange
peels on the window ledge. The riverine sewer fires, thimbles
now, tiny, work themselves almost out.

6.02

The spires rise then turn by turn there is nothing. A propeller and the plane spun behind. Its payload ratchets the embassy loose from the street. Oxidized window tracery. Light gloving through. A man, like cellophane in an old hat. He was clapping erasers together when it happened. With bombing patterns called, cookie cutters and Christmas trees, they seemed to call attention away from drawing.

Detainees broach (consume) an easel's perimeter. Thus space (economy), at any time, is a special aspect, purely substitutional. Perhaps this has nothing to do with that. White cheeks waxed from his jaw, cool against his collar, like a shell. Minimum visibility, it seems, was for him, not enough wanting. The peanut vendor sleeps beneath her cart, but outside is not a place, rather, a reflection. The water remembers you playing *gone* with a stone, a breath. Relax. Capital is permanent, its maintenance taken for granted.

The bridge wears its cables above a cracked menagerie who secrete a certain level of consumption continuously into being. Pinworms, threadbare, cause itching around the anus at night. Soldiers in armored personnel carriers cradle through the pocked streets. Skeletal buildings teeter, described from their girders. You must believe me. In a stationary economy the flow of consumable goods is uniform over time. Eyes border eyes border, perhaps closed—but not every gravity is discreet; no telling which ones will move us.

6.03

Miraculous, tangents full of skies beating — these upset fetuses go to the bodying press, where, with a single stroke, they are stamped with the designs and inscriptions that make them legal, tender bodies. Anchored to her chair, they accord us this latitude. The mapping (s) of which associates domestic investiture with every point (~p).

"Tell me," he says, sipping tea from a tulip and saucer, moth quiet, "tell me a story with smoke in its eyes." Rain, soft at first, approaching, its boots untied, but still the viole( )ts. One set of variables represents instances overcome by mortars. Dozens of box kites pinned to a styrofoam sky: to be lost in a collection of statements, a common law.

They smash the ceiling with their fists, gopher through the hole into the attic. Someone will find her almost overcome, reading a bowed stack of chain letters dedicated to the loneliness of buses. She is in dust. Relief. The moving clock is beyond description.

6.04

Every few seconds the moon projects from a tin can half buried beyond the trees. A bird crosses, scrolling from a player piano, which the lonely ones call mountain. These travelers are tired by now. The river disappears into a keyhole.

The door opens onto a room of rocking chairs, which they know must be assembled. The door puts down its foot behind them. Iambic, it shuts. One woman glues her chair together with mud from the floor. The others are already asleep or on their way, nested in their unfinished constructions, jostling.

She stokes a blessing of fennel under the seat, sits scarved in smoke. All at once, maybe once upon a time, her legs begin to grow. She tries to stand but her legs are already too novel a length, knees too uncertain a mechanism. Pushing her back into the chair, her legs vine along the floor and graft themselves to the windowsill.

6.05

A man in a car twists his handle bar mustache to long, thin points. The car conveys to the man that his door is very much a jar of vinegar. Sauving his left hand along his mustache, pinching the tip sharp with a mastigophoric snap of his fingers, a flourish before his arm, shapeless then determined, darts for the door handle.

As the door slams closed, the window in the door, clumsy as it is, loses its footing, slides into the frame and shatters all the way back to sand. Horseshoe crabs emerge and make their way towards a vinegar wave about to break against that stretch of new beach. Waves crest onto sand.

They neutralize together, bubbling up, up and out of the slot that the window once occupied. This door foam collects finally in a puddle on the street and, as the man watches, shrivels the stones there into raisins. The man begins to cry. I am suggestible, he thinks, or at least easily moved. Yes, that must be it—I am a man who is easily moved by the sudden appearance of raisins.

[digression on the corn trade]

To prepare a chamber, as shown in the figure above, which accommodates even corn's new proportions as compared to a tangle of rebar still rooted amid the tulip-bulbed confluence of a ruptured train car thumbing the circumference of a wound. Sheet rock covers your small embrace.

Slow close up: underarm gushing curls like a derrick. Life-vest salted blue and a recent scarf. Abandoned. Tide to drift wood. He throws off the lights so the planes can land. The number varies inversely, sometimes divisible, sometimes not. Sometimes: tungsten, actinic, strobe — safe.

In some cases, host governments insist on enclosing refugee camps with barbed wire. Our wet souls filled with peanut shells, the runoff governed by an existing barricade. Masquerading as someone else's suit, one of the mourners rubs away the newspaper. Cardinals plot a tractrix, shake free.

7. MULTIPLIER–ACCELERATOR MODEL

7.01

She pretends lost is something you become by coincidence of wants, some dry, others like snow. Is there such a thing as a perfect inflationary cost, an effective communicative model? Aside from the mismatched lip movements, post-synchronized dialogue betrays us. Our tendencies: all tactile, apprehension. We crave the salt of gulls. Evacuate. It's fuzzy here. By degrees, a man said, today—as if history were a tea stained sink. Sparrows this morning and the faucet's steady cough. Standing by the open window, she spools tungsten around an icicle, reaches outside and casts it into the lake.

7.02

Octave or bamboo, just sneak in a prediction. Hand stitched to your shirt's starched collar. To be sleeveless, unarmed. Octave, bamboo. Can you tell us, does hair rust? This morning accounts for (y). Our pours: one by widening one. Polish burnt to a copper vase. Your chipped teeth. "Forget the radon. Hot," you said. Octave. Two hands above a plate of saw dust, thumbs tucked away in the palms. Sand. Stomach. Architect. Forger of guesses and revolts. Static eyed. Station after station. Wet in low wattage. Bamboo. Liquid enigmatist in waist-light. Small breathing.

7.03

Pretend that I want to. In a room furnished with elfin miniatures or the armpit of a woman who refuses revelations. I really don't. I can feel the dawn light. Stop tapping! We are where skies are counted against the death toll. Mortar rejects the brick's wanton pores. A verse of fire ants piles across a bridge wrought of dead scouts.

She shrugged me off and began to swim. You could see her now, but the man that rings the bell doesn't like to shake hands. Forgive him. He rakes leaves into structures and burns them, dances a brutal tango with his rake. Tell me a story that has smoke in its eyes. In the morning, you in transit. My lap, a lantern, relieves these smoldered relics of their contours.

If you persist with this line of questioning, battery powered and ever watchful of Venus in retrograde, the defense will be forced into a charmingly ruckus round of folk songs.

The wet tar cakes apart, sugars boot bottom bees on the go-go. She pollinates. On the corner is a man who beat his shadow into something like a comet. He is guilty of finger-painting; he let the harvest rot in the silo. Please tell me your name, last name last, first name on the dotted line.

7.04

Scorched grazing land like she hunkers. Over a table, pencil in fist, the maps. Taking every point (p) into themselves. She draws, buckled-flat beneath the lamp. Frustrates her elbow's crook. Pearling larger momentarily. Erasures related to the lamplight's hemisphere. Vertigo blows through them. Her abdomen is a forgery, reconfiguration of a dandelion in a wax tray. She records in resin. Cubes the voltage in each of her hairs. Wrist cabled to an escalator clause bearing from its axels. Milk production, notwithstanding. The toll will cost what existed, the act of *going by yourself*. Limestone sparks from punctured bodies in the cornflowers. Tanks asleep. Turret guns swung out blue.

7.05

I am back in our room—that locket—just days before you arrive. It is impossible to taste the difference between you in the morning and apple cider, but where there's a will there's something to be gained and I've got all day and would love another slice of cheesecake. And how did those two get together anyway, cheese and cake? I remember you wore a different shoe on every limb and said something about preferring trains because they are sometimes very late. As a matter of fact, how did we get together?

I have been trying to find you something flat enough to be real, to include; pressed flowers and some glass to keep them sensible. But there is always something winding down between us. A rocking chair, let's say, stamp sized, and then enormous, beside a lake. A man with a low pointed stomach floats on his back, hiding from a seizure of bees. The sky is red and there is a sound like chopping. How are the tremors in your arched topography, my eruption? I will have always chosen the blue wire you know that, even if I cut green. I remember all the hours of ash-light in our vernacular, localized and longing, cracked and without napkins

[digression on the corn trade]

If the corn flops, the bicycles grow almost invisible. Breathing-in larger and larger circles, incognita tend toward infinity and once a day the sea. We run our fingers through the ground: a disquiet, simply. The frequencies of our slouching, also (now dialect or slang) followed by another negative or (chiefly poetic) without preceding negative, are here nor there. We are not meant to be permanent residents.

What linguistic correction, if any, do you expect would vanish agricultural migrancy in this new market? Beyond domestic. Border laborers question high rates of malnutrition, settle into their footprints. The banks have abandoned irrigation development in the border zone due to fractal hostilities. She said, "A few kites have wilted into traffic." You said, "As with the calculation of belief, if you listen far enough, even the slightest departures register."

7.06

We gather under the thinnest sun, peanut colored or burlap.
The radio station has broadcast static for three days, but we
keep dancing just in case the music starts again. Our trajectories
tangle with the latitudes establishing the least expensive model
of communication. Its ashes weighed from a quart of milk, the
charred material transferred to a crucible. Sheet rock covers a
small embrace. This motion defrays its own expense against a
membrane of water. Washed until they ache—skinless—the
doors are conscious of their shadows, what is implied by
degrees. Ruthless simplification along these lines makes the
next construction possible.

7.07

You arrive first as sound and still warm. Black birds corkscrew from treetops, brawl for their limbs. Bulldozers (collective unconscious) phantasmagoric, gear up dust. Refugee camps are usually written in the margins of border cities. Landmines, sedative in this silt. You will have always chosen the blue wire, even when you cut green.

Scripted in avoidance, we abide our various occupations, steal our shoulders and over them. The curfew, somehow lupine, howling up in us, or resembling that structure, i.e. an ideological question, domed.

But to what do(es) you refer? The children process their own angels. Collateral. His small body swims in a blanket that pours between them like plaster. Slowly, as they walk, his ear impresses the fabric's scrim. We leave our doors off the latch, a tacit vigil—leave candles in cans of condensed milk to light their way.

Some of us have developed a rash swarming with occupants (busy) or from which multitudes emerge (peopled). These objects drift. Consider the envoy a moment of congress, ever respectful of artifice, a test-tube stopper tipped forward like a hat. Radio signals counterpoint his every turn, acting to contextualize the economy of a region by its margins. A locomotive unpacks, suddenly. Breaks scale. Your body, too frail to bear, even this slightest current.

8. DEAD LETTER OFFICE

8.01

The smell of honey and smoke prays from the bus as it coughs up passengers. Most of us were hatched in the bread bag factory. Within days the factory vanishes, production capital, what's left of it, sold. Layoffs followed by the bread bags caucusing inside the fence as near money seeds from a car's exhaustoria. Its narrative tires. A lullaby bathes the now empty lot from the window across the street.

A few kites wilt into this traffic carrying every point (p) into themselves but are unable to contain a story that breathes so deeply, moving within it, even the trains are derailed by all the blankets left laying around. She pretends lost is something you become by coincidence of wants. Capital accumulates, always in the joints: trapezium, scaphoid, cuneiform, os magnum — only from a pair, reaching.

8.02

She watches the moon melon and the rind of oaks. At this stage of the manufacturing process the edges of bodies are marked. Her legs, the shutters for the once bare window, take hinge in the frame. Light swallows hard away behind them.

She feels the house, their foundation, arthritic, settle. Afraid, she wants for the others, desires them — wants them to run, but they just watch her struggle. This process is known as reading.

There is applause. You can see it in their eyes. The faucet forgets basin-ward. She has them like a dream. The shutters kick as part of the stamping operation.

Reading intends. A measure, discouraging. The shaving or clipping of bodies was unsanctioned. She opens her mouth and creaks, buttons down her sweater, cradles the others awake.

8.03

There are times when what had been real music swells. We photograph the seaport, afraid to wake. Fanned across a cherry wood table, those images, their inevitable encroachment, capitalization, is memory, no matter how the tankers toggle in.

We are nowhere, hailing. Stone architecture braced against a plate of saw dust. Two hands, thumbs tucked away. A scaffold mewing with strays. Houses near the border have been subject to raids. She combs torpex into her hair in case they come for her. Sunlight flashes between the moths.

Ashes weighed, wet in a low wattage. We guess their diameters from charred material transferred from crucibles. This motion defrays its own expense against quarts of milk. Forget the radon. Marrow is the simplest kind of nightmare. It's the splint, which demands interpretation. Wait for me, please. Folded like a crane.

8.04

We sit by the water fashioning boats from empty ration tins. Absorbing strontium-90 (the lack of what has gone by) plants ramble beneath their potting contaminated with this way not that. This is not a munitions depot but if you act calm you will be calm.

Someone shouts from a wreckage (burrow) of exploded engine parts. The smell of lye because they will never meet. Everything is reversible in this narrow sense of holding. Formally, these bodies associate with an export-led labor model, are perfect haiku. Their omissions (to be) provided by the reader.

Effluvium of toppled bees in the sun. Something churns in a car in a box in a matter of time in terms. Mortars, far off: a pipe, puffed wet. We take turns — seagulls against a chalkboard sky — mapping in dirt, the next place, with sewing needles. We will never arrive.

[digression on the corn trade]

When the corn grows bicycles keel. To keep you warm we
made a map of a product. A spectacle-category, however in
general, develops its burden. Orbits decay. Blade, ticklish rind.
Tremors, at this here-rate, coordinate in the sleeves. You were
long gone.

Every few seconds, three such bendings erase more or less
of the river. Ocher watermark sutured to a lack of vitamins.
Refugee camps are only meant to be a flimsy coat, temporary
index. Beds available per 1000 population and beds used per
1000 population have both constituted output proxies.

You in the corner, on my lap, in a kerosene lantern, a phantom
syntax that sometimes presents wet. Orchids, tangled still.

She sees an infinite rack of stray planets in a garlic clove, lint-
pressed and hipped in a trouser pocket. Pronounced deposits
of fabric on a saddle shaped economy, halved and halved and
have you found the nesting doll's heart or just the air it keeps
from you? The light output is prodigious.

8.05

Driving along a dark road, a man hits something, hearing the collision after hearing the sound of what he will hit being torn free. He stops, checks the front of his car, a badger paw lodged in the grill. Each object here is thickly sown with identical clocks synchronized by a radio signal. The turn signal signals a counter point to the crickets. As the moving clock travels through this territory, its reading at any particular point is compared. He tries to feel for this stationary clock, but he can't. Regret is too similar a time/position, growing denser by degrees. To procure a confession, they grate his hand against a fence when the sun goes down, sheer, almost bone. A likeness, creased.

In the morning, he unspools two lengths of red yarn each the length of his arm, which he promptly cuts off below the shoulder and throws in the trash. The measured survival fraction provides information about elapsed time. Seconds clot between his shoulder and the floor. In this specific, statistical, sense (he) is a kind of clock: he repeats. This operation may be taken as a measure of the interval between successive ticks of our particulars or our disconnections in any given space. The moon reconfigures his face, closes his eyes. He imagines the yarn is his last story of muscle. The paw, tethered to that story, swings heavy against his side, interrupting the flies' meticulous redactions.

8.06

Small lanterns in branches. An old man buries a wreath of
gladiolas. Tailpipe. Tea kettle. Breadth. Freight trains debate
their tracks. Fertilizer deposits piggyback on a tomato. Or
seeming now to rain now he starts to warm. Hum of an old
television. A room balloons. Beyond its sills. A nightgown of
mosquitoes. Their bodies nova in the headlights.

Latex gloves, wet, full with fingers. His face traces, is traced.
Sediments. Said amounts, catalogued in an oak's concentric
longings. Even thirsty, how quite they are? Light blistering
from these point objects after refraction in a particular. Your
hands could be so sincere sometimes. But why does move over
always mean away? Herons paper and unpaper their wings.
Too often transparency gives pause for infection. Gives the
joints reason. The spoor is called cryptosporidium. Thimbles
like toppled statuary, on the window ledge. A riverine sewer
fire peels orange.

9. THE VELOCITY OF A BODY TOGETHER

9.01

I went with a friend for a drink. Two men approached, watering cans hoisted in the parabolas of their arms, and asked my friend along with them. I waited and waited. Soybeans all lit up with frost. I never found him again. Some of us looked for his proxy, his other shoulders, the ones that delivered quietly. But nothing else came to shore, girdled or otherwise prosthetic.

The bodies of the disappeared, recalcitrant within the body politic, are rhetorical, that is to say (dis)figurative. Cattle graze in tall grass, refer commuters to the substances they synthesize. There's no authority in it. In a sense we can only imply. Silk lilacs shadowed by two high walls.

Soon after, my wife was found lashed to stop sign, beetles marching off with her softer parts. They didn't allow us to bury her. There was manioc flour in her hair, creased in her seams, but no matter how I write the story, it always reads like obsession.

9.02

Our window is a fixative, six cents worth, and for me it dries always the same. Slippery in the estuaries of your hands, an ebbing proprioception littered with whittled biscuits qua follow me please. Employing a powdered soap, rumored to prevent, I wash the map where it folds. Your departure pearls in the moss-necklaced trees.

Each time we move the water feels different. Sleep tastes like bleach here. Refugees should be able to stand in all areas of the tent without hitting their heads on the ceiling. When a citizen crosses a body of water, it is said, they afford it. Goods on the other hand are re-venued.

Commercial traffic has been mapped out. Secreted as to translate. An organ grinder cranks this desire, which extends a shadow, paging toward plot. You scale, sinuous, up a cliff where your dog already sits, shaking, all its toys packed up in a cart that conveys also his hind legs. "Stop being so melodramatic," you say. "Come to the river."

9.03

Night-blooming cereus crowds an iron-worked window white. Her legs creak the shutter's sanctions. Hinges of loose light trade routes with our bodies, the floor.

A butterfly or butterfly chair eats itself blue. For a struck matchbook of evenings, cork-soled dancers keep the owls at bay. I have always loved to dance and it seems that real wages can go even further virtually unchanged since the innerspring mattress was invented in 1925. At that moment I was at the river, doing laundry.

Clearly we are now embedded in complex questions of timing. I heard the gunshots. The doors easily ajar. Nervous for the others — desiring them — wanting them to run. Their collisions spark; eyes pretend together, retreat sadly. Fortunately I found some money in a pair of trousers. To avoid detection, he quiets the infant's cough with opium. I didn't look for my mother.

Milkweed like a fever we move through. Very fine particles released. After collapse. The velocity of a body — together.

9.04

A whisper is not a place, rather a reflection anchored in fleeting currents — like that. And that's how we lived. We wished across each other's hands with stones, played evacuation games. Beautiful arms. Seceding catapults. Our consumptions measured in the depth an explosion produced, its rate of disupholstery. You and I invested that teapot with our lint pressed correspondence. Crop duster's goggles, powdered milk, once you even stuffed yourself inside. Each letter you wrote was a re-semblance of the last. I heard they found you, soaked apart like paper in the rain, that you lost yourself at the masquerade. There is a truck waiting for you somewhere, blue and white like unpuzzled sky, and I'm afraid you will climb in to solve it.

[digression on the corn trade]

When the corn grows a pair of boots, fills with rain, the expense of transporting one part of the city to another increases. I remember you, remember your proportions weighted against what you knew of dreaming. You spread a liberal amount of paste over a small area not possible in an ordinary three-dimensional space and assumed that object real. Pointed to it. A point in space related, orthogonally, to you, addressed with ribs torn from the folds of a yellow coat.

In the distance, refrigerated train cars couple east. You are somewhere by now, hair parted just so, pocket watch fused to your hip, feeling crowed from the inside. I think you ran away, a survivor's exile. But the suggestion of burnt hair and garlic is a part of you now. No distance of track, no amount of honeysuckle, can ease your breathing. You told me that after the explosion everything went quiet, that the silence was palpable. Nevertheless, you hear them scream while you sleep, see yourself in the third person, static, ogling the blaze. Two little thermometers, suspended so as not to touch.

Above the city, sound occupies a different duration, my love, like weather. Words catalogued in raindrops. I hear them too—the echoes—when it pours, their cacophonous release as they collide with things. I get lonely after they evaporate. But the wind is still kind, recognizes how lost we are, is the only thing left that asks after us.

9.05

Muskmelon rinds sulfur in the wreckage of an apartment house, mortared. Walls scrubbed until they ache. The bodies are there, after all, to accommodate the insulation. Tents should be covered with an outer fly to shade and protect the tent below. Hummock of porcelain basins, ulcerous—that weight. The hungry wring away. Would it have been enough to have said tourniquet, wet in a maple? Her jacket frames a cedar push of breath. Seconds clot between her.

Relax, close your eyes, your law enforcement organs are functioning normally. What we saw at the time (t) on our clock represents the reading. In her home (the term not the thing committed) the moving clock, at some earlier time, was the distance of that clock from us. She sponges his small body, what remains, with dish soap, says sorry, then again. In the washbasin, the clock collapses toward us, inequitable as memory. This focal cluster is a collection of linguistic nodes with varying functionality all subserving a common representation. To swarm (hoard), to swarm (siphon) off, to hail another, as to be, for the first time, seen.

9.06

How long has it been since you unlaced your shoes and emptied the pebbles? Is your coffee sweet enough? Have you found him? I hear he's been listening to radio static, huffing gasoline when he finds it. I remember when we worked the refinery. There were birthmarks on his washcloth. That cough, our common index. You never looked in the mirror then. None of us did. But I think he misses it, the refinery, misses those days away from the sun. Tomorrow we will stop searching, look at things through trees again or gates, through ropes, flimsy curtains. I know where they keep the blindfolds. Anything's better than walking backward through someone else's life. A bus smokes past, and from it, a little crowded prayer crescendos: *Hush now, baby. Soon done.*

Someone once told me, there are only two kinds of stories. A man goes on a trip or a stranger comes to town. We are the remainders. Counting the numbers of steps bottled in bodies. I wonder how many that woman has left? She ladles honey with her fingers; the three longest, knuckle-deep, lashed tight together, braces the jar against her chin. Chicken wire hatches every window. I thought I saw him yesterday, eating himself bald near a sluice but all I could think to say was *steam* and his ship was already too far.

9.07

Our reservoir despairs. Drawn & quartered. Slate masquerading
in moss. Geese shake. Free their wet souls. Parking lot. I
am responsible to the runoff. Clearing the autumn drain.
Florescent. Dye maps your sentence through. The karst towers
and my hair is not long enough. To be rescued. Bed springs
weaving. My spine. That mercy: acetylene blousing a girder.

I found pictures of us. Amid the wasps. Your flight at 6:15.
We can find and lose the earth here. Breath. Isn't invisible. You
say, "scaffolding." Our relief tendered from a single glacier. All
this rain, transgressing. Called back into being and being lost.

9.08

In an overgrown trance of wisteria and downed birds we are making for the hills like a rhapsody. Always running toward a starting. Pistols, drawn lacquer, behind us, a sentence, which leaves our hands. Delimitations are only averages. Away in the sun we reach velocity. Children armed with compasses drawing circles over circles until everything is laced to a point of departure, only grayer. But still our bodies interpret, interrupt, the creaks of angels as they iris groundward from their halos. Cheek cells scraped onto a slide, dyed with iodine, and filled with light. And is this the story of bodies or the story of light? And who tells it? Is it you? Do you remember your first miracle? Window after window, we were the voices under all that glass.

.

.

.